THE PELICAN HISTORY OF ART

EDITED BY NIKOLAUS PEVSNER

z28

ART AND ARCHITECTURE IN ITALY: 1250–1400

JOHN WHITE

Simone Martini: St Louis of Toulouse, 1317.
Naples, Galleria Nazionale

JOHN WHITE

ART AND ARCHITECTURE IN ITALY

1250 TO 1400

· HISTORY · PELICAN · THE · OF · ART ·

PUBLISHED BY PENGUIN BOOKS

Penguin Books Ltd, Harmondsworth, Middlesex
Penguin Books Inc., Baltimore, Maryland, U.S.A.
Penguin Books Pty Ltd, Ringwood, Victoria, Australia

*

Copyright © John White, 1966
First published 1966

*

Text printed by Richard Clay (The Chaucer Press), Ltd, Bungay, Suffolk
Plates printed by Lund Humphries & Co. Ltd, Bradford
Made and printed in Great Britain

TO

XENIA WHITE

*

CONTENTS

CONTENTS

Part Two

Sculpture: 1250–1300

Part Three

Painting: 1250–1300